Your Dog's Grandmother

Sage Advice for the Modern Canine

by Grandma Pippy with CM Marihugh

Your Dog's Grandmother

Sage Advice for the Modern Canine

by Grandma Pippy with CM Marihugh

Dear Canine, Are you challenged to behave properly in public? Do you find yourself embarrassed in social situations because of your lack of ettiquette?

Your troubles are over because of a WONDERFUL new book! This volume holds the WISDOM of the ages! It has counsel on living from past generations. Who else knows more about life than those who have lived it? Especially, as it relates to co-existing with our "best friends" - those two-legged creatures who can be so hard to please.

The creator, Grandma Pippy, wanted to find a way to HELP the canine family of the future. Herself a mother of 42, she knows the value of the GOOD ADVICE she received. So, she called on her sagest friends to tap their experience. Now you can REAP THE BENEFIT of this collected knowledge!

No more need to pay big dollars for those tired training courses. Who among us needs one more hour of being told how to sit, stand, fetch, and so on?

It's time to get the real thing! Whether you struggle with the everyday situations of life, or are just looking for new ways to find contentment in living, this book is waiting to CURE ALL YOUR DIFFICULTIES! Pick one up today at your quality bookshop!

"My discomfort in social situations was making me desperate and depressed. Then I heard about this invaluable book and it has changed my life!" -Tuffy

"As new parents, we were helpless trying to convey important life lessons. The we got this treasure chest of a book! It has given us so much good guidance to pass on to our pups!" -Minnie and Rover

August 24, 1912

Dear Reader,

   For some time, an important matter weighed
heavily on my heart. I had been thinking about my
descendants. This world is changing faster and
faster. How could I help my future family live
more happily?
   I feared not only for my own grandchildren
and great-grandchildren, but for all those of the
canine persuasion. Where would they get their morals?
Their values? Their sense of duty to their masters
and mistresses? How would they learn to sweetly
yet firmly hold sway over humans? It is well known
our protectors are strange creatures, but living in
kinship with them is the best way for a happy life!
   Well, I gave it long and thoughtful deliberation.
And bless my soul, if it didn't come to me when my
mistress told me to sit for the millionth time. Why
not ask some of my oldest and wisest friends to
share their sage advice with the canines to come?
   The happy result is this book, dear Reader. It holds
valuable instruction from your forebears. They each
selected a photo to illustrate a life lesson. And
it's commonsense counsel — no highfalutin jabber here!
I begin the book with one of my own tips for living.
   I encourage you to read and take heed, listen and
learn! Strive for excellence! And most of all,
be happy!

I remain your dearest,

Grandma Pippy

☞ No.1

Grandma Pippy, 1912

You must learn to make your opinion known at the proper time. Why, I sat so nice and quiet for this picture all gussied up.
Then, on the way out I bit the photographer, and when we got home, I peed on the rug. I think I made my point.

☞ No.2

Grandmother Sadie, 1911

☞ No.3

Granddad Mike,1907

Maintain control at all times. As in right now, I'm dying to go berserk. Chew thru this cockamamie bow whatchamacallit. Bite this joker's hand. Then hightail,hear me? Just hightail!
BUT NO SIR! I AM STICKIN' WITH! Buckin'up. Facin'the squad. Bitin'the bullet.
(and lemme tell ya, this ain't no happy sailor)

☞ No.4

Great Grandma Tilly, 1906

Did you girls see Mopsie's new do? 'course, I won't say a word!
Yep. Still looks like she stuck a paw in the electricity.
Looks like a blimp on her head?
If you can be still while gossip and rumors fly, well, you'll be a grown-up pooch, Dear.

☛ No.5

Old Grandpa Jack, 1910

☞ No.6

Grand-Mama Hazel, 1907

Bring joy into this world!! It doesn't matter if you're playing in a pretend band in a painted forest! What matters is chuckles! What matters is giggles! What matters is smiles!
somebody please get me out of this nightmare

☞ No.7

Auntie Belle & Uncle Billy, 1908

Bear all with silent grace and dignity.
No matter how darn humiliatin'
(x*@z*#!*#)

☛ No.8

Grandpa Max, 1912

Remember, your place is by the Master's side thru thick and thin. Even if he's daffy-looking, 3rd-tier royalty, you must stick by him!
COUNT DE BEAUFORT

☛ No.9

Great Aunt Fluffy, 1909

You must tell the truth. Lil' Louise always asks me if she looks pretty and I woof, "Nope."
Just ignores me- poor little sap. Never can see the curls don't help much.

☞ No.10

Grandpappy Jake, 1910

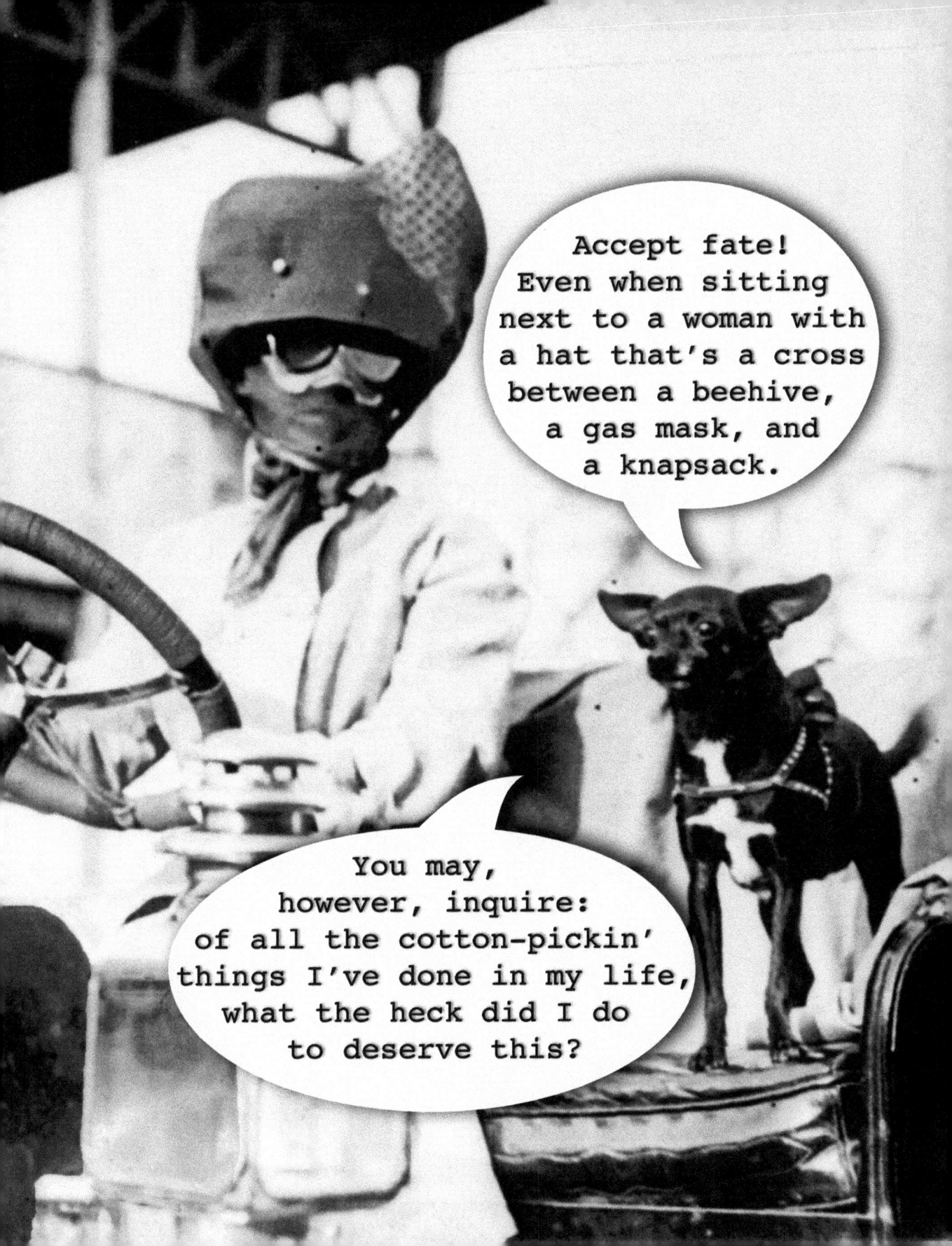

☞ No.11

Great Grandpa Fido, 1908

1ST PATIENT, DOG HOSPITAL, N.Y. CITY
At some time, you may be asked to be a Pioneer, a Forerunner, a Hero! You may be called to greatness!
You must then remember your higher self! Don't blow it all by snarlin' or peein' or whinin' or barin'your teeth or some other durn thing like that.

☞ No.12

Great Grand-Mama Tiffany, 1912

My dears! Spread the art of tasteful fashion whenever you can! I often teach Miss Penelope by chewing up ghastly shoes, ripping apart vile dresses, and hiding dreadful hats.
Well.
No one can say I don't try.

☛ No.13

Grandpa Pal, 1914

Be nice to kids. The lil' punks can drive ya nuts, but they're always dropping food all over the place.

☞ No.14

Grandfather Gustav, 1900

☞ No. 15

Grandpa's Nigel,Henry,Eddie,&George,1910

MAJ. RICHARDSON & BRITISH RED CROSS DOGS
I say, our troupe is a great group o'chaps - jolly good! One for all and all for one!
So stick with the pack, mates. 'Specially if you got a piece o'work in charge. Call ours Major Dingbat-son.
guy's a bleedin'idiot
bloomin' josser

☞ No.16

Aunt Bijou & Uncle Diablo, 1905

Remember, never fear your mistress.
Unless she looks pretty frightening! Ha-ha-ha! Thank heavens for netting! Ha-ha-ha!
oh shut-up, you old fool.

☞ No.17

Great Uncle Buster & Grandpa Ben, 1909

Remember that your friends won't listen to ya. I told him, once you let 'em put that cap on, all tarnation's gonna break loose! But nooooo, he had to be Mr. Nice Guy: "Ah Buster, where's the harm?"
And I say, Stick by your decisions. Don't listen to all the Mr.I-told-you-so's! Make a mistake? Put up with the consequences in style!

☛ No. 18

Grandfather Scipio, 1907

CM Marihugh

CM Marihugh preserves histories and creates legacies for individuals, families, and organizations. She records these heirloom stories in artful video, audio, and print. Her love of history, legacies, and dogs led her to this project with Grandma Pippy. CM hopes that canines will appreciate the words of their forebears a little more than their best friends seem to! (particularly her own canines)

As a personal historian, CM has interviewed and recorded many to preserve their life stories for their families. She holds seminars on life story writing. Her goal is to encourage all to preserve their histories for themselves and future generations. A native Vermonter, CM has lived and worked in many parts of the world. She now enjoys more sunshine while living in Austin. CM@CMMarihugh.com

www.ingramcontent.com/pod-product-compliance
Lightning Source LLC
LaVergne TN
LVHW061221060426
835508LV00014B/1392